Published by Creative Education
P.O. Box 227, Mankato, Minnesota 56002
Creative Education is an imprint of The Creative Company
www.thecreativecompany.us

Design by Stephanie Blumenthal
Production by Christine Vanderbeek
Art direction by Rita Marshall
Printed in the United States of America

Photographs by Alamy (Mary Evans Picture Library), Corbis (Ted Spiegel,
Stapleton Collection, Bo Zaunders), Dreamstime (Stasyuk Stanislav), Getty
Images (Tom Dahlin, Liz McAulay, National Geographic, STEFFEN ORTMANN/
AFP, Popperfoto), iStockphoto (Zbynek Burival, Andrew J Shearer, SOMATUSCANI,
Duncan Walker, Casper Wilkens, ZU_09), Mary Evans Picture Library, Shutterstock
(J. Helgason), Superstock (age footstock, Bridgeman Art Library, London, Fine
Art Photographic Library, Robert Harding Picture Library, Image Asset
Management Ltd., Pantheon, Prisma, Universal Images Group)

Library of Congress Cataloging-in-Publication Data
Gunderson, Jessica.
Vikings / by Jessica Gunderson.
p. cm. — (Fearsome fighters)
Summary: A compelling look at the Vikings, including the ways they terrorized
western Europe, their lifestyle, their weapons, and how they remain a part of today's
culture through books and film.
Includes bibliographical references and index.
ISBN 978-1-60818-185-8
1. Vikings—Juvenile literature. I. Title.

DL66.G87 2012
948'.022—dc23   2011035801

First edition
2 4 6 8 9 7 5 3 1

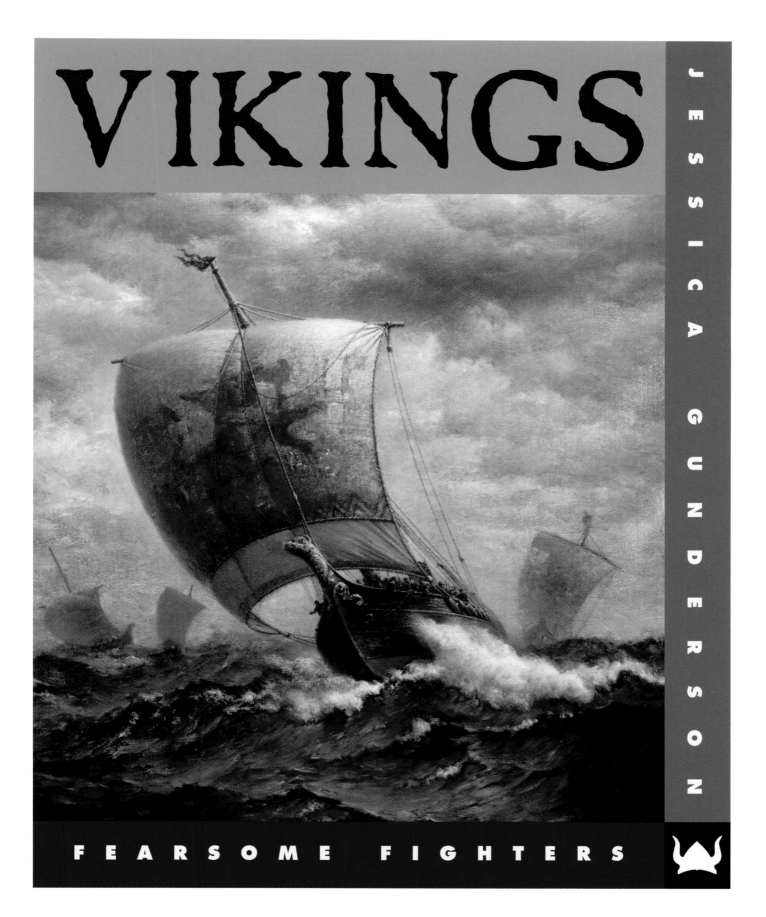

VIKINGS

JESSICA GUNDERSON

FEARSOME FIGHTERS

CREATIVE EDUCATION

From the beginning of time, wherever groups of people have lived together, they have also fought among themselves. Some have fought for control of basic necessities—food, water, and shelter—or territory. Others have been spurred to fight by religious differences. Still others have fought solely for sport. Throughout the ages, some fighters have taken up arms willingly; others have been forced into battle. For all, however, the ultimate goal has always been victory.

For nearly three centuries, ferocious Viking warriors, hungry for riches and territory, sailed the seas in their majestic longships, terrorizing coastal villages and Christian **monasteries**. Wearing helmets and wielding swords and battle-axes, these Scandinavian warriors stormed the quiet countryside, seizing captives, valuables, and cities. During the dark winter months, many Viking warriors lived peaceful lives as farmers in their homelands, but once spring arrived, they would embark upon dangerous journeys to foreign lands. Sometimes they would never return home again, instead settling in places they'd invaded. Although the Vikings have long since disappeared from the seas, stories of their distant adventures and violent escapades have allowed them to sail on in our imaginations.

THE DAWN OF THE VIKING AGE

On June 8, 793 A.D., a Viking longship sailed quietly along the northern coasts of the British Isles and dropped anchor at Lindisfarne. Viking warriors poured from the ship and stormed the sleepy Lindisfarne monastery. They wreaked havoc upon the island, stealing valuables such as statues, fabric, and jewels and capturing fleeing monks to sell into slavery. The Lindisfarne raid was the Vikings' first upon Britain, but it would not be their last. From the late 8th century to the 11th, Viking longships would dominate European seas, striking fear into the hearts of all who saw the ships' silhouette on the horizon. The Viking Age had begun.

More than 300 years before the raid at Lindisfarne, the Roman Empire—which once ruled much of Europe, northern Africa, and parts of Asia—had collapsed, opening trade between the Middle East, Europe, and Russia. Tribes of people **migrated** across mainland Europe in search of trade, work, and land. At that time, the present-day Scandinavian countries of Norway, Sweden, Denmark, and Finland were controlled by many chieftains who owned large chunks of land and had their own small armies. During the so-called migration period, Scandinavia became exposed to the goods and riches of other cultures and regions. Scandinavian merchants desired gold, silk, spices, and wine, while traders from the south coveted Scandinavian bearskins, reindeer hides, furs, and ivory from walrus tusks.

Scandinavian advancements in seafaring and shipbuilding bolstered trade. Scandinavia was a land of water. Norway had an expanse of coastal lands and **fjords**, Denmark had a multitude of islands, and Sweden and Finland featured numerous inland lakes and rivers in addition to their coasts. For centuries, Scandinavian people had been closely tied to the sea, sailing often

THE VIKINGS SAILED WIDELY TO FIGHT, PILLAGE, AND SETTLE, COMING INTO CONFLICT WITH AN ARRAY OF PEOPLES

upon its waves to fish or travel. In the late 700s, the development of the longship, which could sail greater distances and carry more cargo than the ships that preceded it, helped trade flourish between Scandinavia and its southern neighbors.

As trade expanded, Scandinavians sought more wealth and land, and, using their knowledge of the high seas, adventurous men hoisted sails in their sturdy ships and headed for other lands in search of riches. They were going *a-viking*, a phrase which meant "to voyage" and was soon used to describe these Scandinavian raiders. The Vikings scoured the British and Irish coasts, initially targeting mainly poorly guarded monasteries, which could be easily plundered.

The British Isles, made up of a collection of divided and warring kingdoms, were especially susceptible to Viking raids, as were present-day France and the Netherlands. Vikings from the various Scandinavian regions attacked areas in proximity. Danish Vikings sailed inland along France's Seine River, laying **siege** to the town of Paris and claiming lands. Meanwhile, warriors from Sweden turned their attention east to what is now Russia, capturing slaves there and trading with merchants. As the Viking Age went on and Viking shipbuilding continued to improve, Scandinavian warriors set their sights on more distant targets, sailing as far south as the Mediterranean Sea and North Africa. In the late

THE VIKINGS' SKILLS IN NAVIGATING THE SEAS WERE EVERY BIT AS IMPRESSIVE AS THEIR SKILLS IN WAGING WAR

$\mathcal{U}$ntil the 12th century, Scandinavians' written language used letters or symbols called runes, which were also used in various Germanic languages of the time. The Scandinavian alphabet (called futhark *after the first 6 letters—*f, u, th, a, r, *and* k) consisted of 16 runes, each of which represented a sound in the spoken language. The Vikings believed runes were a gift from the god Odin, and they regarded the symbols with awe and reverence, not inscribing them casually. Runes were most often carved upon gravestones to honor the dead. Runic inscriptions have been found throughout Europe, Russia, and other places Vikings fought or settled.

VIKINGS

900s, near the end of the Viking Age, Norwegian Vikings set sail for the largely uninhabited lands of Iceland and Greenland, not to fight and pillage but to settle.

Life at sea was not easy for Viking warriors. Although the "Northmen," as they were commonly called, were expert sailors, deadly shipwrecks were not uncommon. At night, Vikings beached their ship if they were close to land and set up camp along the shore, but if they were on the open sea, they slept on the ship's deck, often in two-person sleeping bags made of sealskin for warmth. On the open deck of a longship, Vikings were exposed to all kinds of harsh weather—rain, winds, and even snow—and were cold and damp much of the time. Sickness was rampant and, because of the conditions, difficult to overcome. If a Viking warrior died, he was likely to be thrown into the sea. Viking voyages lasted several months or sometimes even years, and a Viking ship often returned home at the end of a journey carrying significantly fewer warriors than when it had set sail.

The common stereotype of a Viking warrior is largely unflattering, his image through the ages that of an **illiterate** and uncivilized brute. However, many Vikings were only part-time warriors and full-time landowners who, for many months of the year, lived at home with their families and oversaw the workings of their farms. Scandinavian farms were large, **self-sustaining**, and often isolated, requiring much work by the Vikings' thralls—slaves who had either been captured on raids or were born into the role. Viking families, along with their thralls, lived in communal longhouses made of wood, with a single room 40 feet (12 m) or more in length. A fiery hearth glowed in the center of the room and provided heat and light, and the meat of wild game or domestic livestock was roasted on a spit over the flames. Longhouses had no windows and only one chimney, and the air inside the house was often smoky, dark, and stale. Benches lined the walls, and at night, everyone slept on the floor around the hearth. Once or twice a year, a Viking landowner would

Meat and fish made up a large part of the Scandinavian diet in the Viking Age. It was typically smoked, dried, or salted so it would keep through the long winter months and on Viking expeditions. Scandinavians grew their own vegetables, such as peas, beans, root vegetables, and cabbage, as well as cereal crops such as barley, rye, and oats. Berries and wild game were harvested from nearby forests, and cheese was made from the milk of cows, sheep, and goats. Meals were accompanied by ale (made from barley) and mead (made from fermented honey), often drunk from a drinking horn.

be called to an assembly meeting known as a "thing," in which all free men from the area would gather to discuss governing issues such as landowner rights or the punishment of criminals.

Vikings were quickly labeled **pagans** and enemies of Christianity. However, their attacks upon monasteries were not necessarily attacks against Christianity. Monasteries were simply easy, unguarded targets that contained riches such as offerings, wine, and religious statues made of precious metals. Vikings, though not Christian like most of their Western European neighbors, did uphold many religious beliefs and worshiped numerous gods. Odin was the Viking god of poetry, magic, and war. Also called the Alfather, Odin had great power and knowledge, and Vikings offered sacrifices and prayers to him before setting forth on voyages. Thor, another revered Viking god whose name was derived from the Old Norse word for "thunder," wielded a hammer and was the god of storms, strength, and destruction. Freyja was worshiped as the goddess of fertility and love, and Njord, Freyja's father, was said to bring good fortune to seafarers and hunters.

While their Viking husbands were away at sea, women assumed responsibility for the farm and its workings. Scandinavian women enjoyed more freedoms and rights than many women of other cultures during that time and were respected in society. Scandinavian women had the right to own land and obtain a divorce, unlike most European women. Many Vikings practiced **polygamy** and had several wives living and working together in the family longhouse.

Scandinavian winters are cold, long, and dark, and during the winter months, Viking families spent much of their time indoors. Men planned expeditions, and poets, called skalds, entertained with stories of Viking adventures. Children listened to the skalds' tales and longed to someday become warriors, too. At age 12, boys were considered men, and many hopped aboard Viking ships bound to conduct *strandhoggs* (coastal raids). Often, they returned some years later to become family men or landowners, either giving up pillaging completely or spending only part of their time on Viking expeditions.

IN VIKING LORE, THE GOD ODIN IS PORTRAYED AS AN AGING BUT POWERFUL FIGURE WITH THE CLASSIC NORDIC BEARD

THE WAY OF THE WARRIOR

The Viking code instructed a warrior to be cautious and prepared at all times, and he adhered to such rules as "look carefully around doorways before entering" and "always keep weapons within reach." Every Scandinavian man, whether he went on seafaring raids or not, had to be ready and able to fight, and that meant being armed. Even when he was in the fields or calling upon neighbors, he would carry at least a knife.

In popular culture, a Viking warrior is often portrayed carrying a battle-ax. Although a Viking did often wield an ax, his weapon of choice was typically a long, double-edged sword, which he used to hack at his enemies. Because a warrior needed to be able to switch from hand to hand easily during battle, either for better aim or in case of injury to one arm, the sword had to be light in weight with a graspable hilt. A Viking took special care of his sword, and each was unique to its owner. The sword's hilt was engraved with runic symbols and images. Some swords had a special name engraved upon them, such as *Gramr* (Fierce) and *Fotbitr* (Foot-biter), to depict the qualities of its owner. A Viking prized his sword and was either buried with it or passed it on to a son.

Bows and arrows were useful to warriors fighting from their ships or storming a fortified city or castle. According to popular legends, the strings of Viking bows were woven from women's hair, but in truth, strings were likely made from linen. Vikings also used two types of spears—a javelin for throwing in long-range attacks and a lance for thrusting attacks. A spear's iron blade could be up to two feet (61 cm) long and was mounted on a wooden shaft six to nine feet (1.8–2.7 m) in length.

To deflect any weapons an opponent might bring against him, a Viking carried a

A CLOSE LOOK AT THE HANDLE OF AN IRON VIKING SWORD, SHOWING THE ORNATE CARVINGS ON THE WEAPON'S HILT

shield made of hardwood—often linden—with reinforced iron panels. The shield could be circular or kite-shaped and was at least three feet (91 cm) in diameter to protect the upper body. Shields were often hung around the neck to leave a Viking's hands free for fighting.

A warrior never went into battle without a helmet, although **archaeological** evidence suggests that the typical Viking helmet was not horned, as is often depicted in popular culture. Instead, it was usually a conical cap made of iron, with a plain leather or iron nose guard. While horned Viking helmets may have existed, such headwear was probably used only in religious rituals worshiping Odin. A Viking's usual attire was a wool tunic and trousers, along with a leather-padded breastplate for protection in battle. Wealthier Vikings wore shirts of **chain mail** for better protection.

Armor and weapons were valuable to the Vikings, but ultimately, the Northmen's power and success was due to their longships. For more than 1,000 years before the Viking Age began, Scandinavians had been making innovations in

shipbuilding. Scandinavians sailed in various types of ships, but the longship was preferred for warring expeditions. The largest of these longships was called a *drakkar* (dragonship), so named because of the dragon's head engraved upon the **prow** to ward off sea monsters or evil spirits. Built for speed and agility, the longship was lighter and handled better than English or French ships of the time. The Viking longship was unique in that it had an identical bow (front) and stern (back), which allowed the sailors to reverse course easily without turning the ship around—all they had to do was change the direction of their rowing. Another essential aspect of the vessel's design was its low draft, or distance between the waterline and the bottom of the **hull**. This structural feature allowed it to sail not only upon the deep waters of the ocean but also on shallow rivers without risk of getting bogged down.

Vikings maneuvered a longship using a steering oar that was attached to the starboard, or right-hand, side of the boat. Like other ships of the time, Viking longships used sails to catch

*V*iking leaders often had groups of berserkers in their armies. Berserkers were fearsome warriors who wore
bearskin shirts called berserks. *Before going into battle, the berserkers would hold a ritual for Odin, whirling and danc-
ing until they were so frenzied they believed they could feel no pain. In their agitated state, the berserkers would then
rush onto the battlefield. Just the sight of their crazed eyes and bearskin attire was enough to fill enemies with dread.
The phrase "going berserk" is used today to describe someone who is out of control.*

wind for propulsion. A longship moved with just one large woolen sail, often red or red-and-white striped and more than 330 square feet (31 sq m) in size. A long, diagonal wooden rod called a spar at the sail's corner allowed the crew to make adjustments if strong winds developed. Decked out with a full outfit of oars, a longship could traverse without wind as well. An 80-foot (24 m) longship carried 80 to 100 men and had about 50 oars, which Vikings rowed in shifts.

Master shipbuilders hired a team of workers to build a longship. Choosing the proper type and shape of tree for various aspects of the ship was essential. Tall, straight trees, usually oaks, were needed for long **keels**. Trees with natural bends or twists were chosen to create the curved bottoms of the boat. The shipbuilder overlapped the planks, attaching them with iron nails or wooden pegs, and the gaps were sealed with tar or caulking. This so-called "clinker" method of boatbuilding gave the hulls some flexibility, allowing them to bend rather than break in strong waves. After the ship was finished, skilled **artisans** carved the dragonhead on the prow as well as intricate patterning on the sides.

A good ship was so important to a Viking leader that, upon his death, he would be buried in it, along with his weapons and sometimes his horse or dog. Vikings believed that the ship would help the chieftain sail into the afterlife. Sometimes the boat was set out to sea with the dead man upon its deck, but more often, the entire ship and its contents were buried in enormous graves on land.

In addition to being warriors, Vikings had to be expert sailors, and they developed several **nautical** techniques to help guide them across the waters. They often sailed within sight of land and used landmarks to keep track of their course and to guide them on their return voyage. They relied on the positions of the sun and stars to tell them which direction they were heading. If it was cloudy, sailors may have used a stone made of feldspar, a mineral that amplifies light. When held to the sky, the stone could indicate the sun's direction. Viking sailors also took note of birds and sea creatures to help assess their position; for example, the narwhal, a toothed whale, is found only in the Arctic, so if one was sighted, a Viking would know he was in the Arctic seas.

The Oseberg ship burial in Norway dates back to 834 and reveals a wealth of artifacts from the Viking Age. The grave was that of a woman, probably a princess or queen, who was buried in an elegant ship along with a female companion (possibly a slave), a wagon, 4 **sledges**, 12 horses, an ox, a tent, food, 5 beds, a chair, a **tapestry**, and many other goods and utensils. The presence of food and supplies illustrates the Viking belief that the dead undertake long journeys to the afterlife. The ship and some of its contents are today on display at the Viking Ship Museum in Oslo, Norway.

FIGHTING, BY LAND AND BY SEA

Viking warriors often came from good families and had been preparing for warfare since boyhood. Boys would engage in activities such as climbing steep mountains and swimming in icy waters to condition themselves to physically demanding environments. Children learned to use weapons at a young age, and they practiced handling swords and spears and shooting bows and arrows.

Viking battles occurred at home as well as abroad, at sea and on land. Feuds between rival Viking chieftains sometimes called a warrior's fighting skills into play. Each chieftain had an elite unit of about 50 to 100 warriors called a lith. Warriors within the lith had a strong fellowship with each other. A chieftain did not have to exert much discipline to keep his Vikings in place; the Viking sense of honor and loyalty was enough. A true Viking warrior would never abandon his leader or his lith, even in the most intense battles.

Warriors within the chieftain's lith were loyal to the death, but the units were actually rather temporary alliances. When an overseas campaign concluded, the warriors dispersed. Some of them returned to their homes in Scandinavia; others joined other liths or gathered their own groups and set off to explore.

Viking ships sailed in fleets that, depending on the length and scale of a mission, could include anywhere from 3 vessels to more than 100. When it was time for the fleet to depart, the shields suspended from the rails on each boat were drawn up and stowed. The sailors raised the gangplank and took their places at the oars, using their trunks of belongings as seats. They rowed until the winds of the open sea allowed them to raise their sails, and thus they traveled until reaching the destination of their first raid.

A typical Viking raid relied upon the element of surprise. Victims had no way of knowing

FROM BOYHOOD TO DEATH, A SCANDINAVIAN MALE WAS EXPECTED TO EMBRACE COMBAT AND A SEAGOING WAY OF LIFE

*T*he sites of four Viking military camps have been discovered in Denmark. Dating back to 980, the camps were likely built during King Harald Bluetooth's campaign to unite Denmark. The camps were forts surrounded by a circular, earthen wall reinforced with wood. Trelleborg, on the island of Zeeland, measured 446 feet (136 m) in diameter. This camp was protected by double walls and a water-filled ditch. The fort was divided into quadrants, and each quadrant held 4 houses, each 100 feet (30 m) long, arranged in a square. The buildings show no sign of having been repaired, suggesting the camps were probably used for no longer than about 30 years.

the Northmen were approaching until the ships appeared on the horizon, their striped flags and dragon-headed prows a telltale sign of what was to come. But by that time, it was too late. The Viking ships quickly approached the shore, and warriors stampeded the beach to attack. They captured people and livestock, gathered gold and other valuables, and set fire to buildings. As a cunning strategy, Vikings often attacked on Sundays and religious holidays, knowing that the inhabitants would be occupied in ceremony and thus unprepared to defend themselves.

Vikings weren't always prowling for blood, however. Especially on longer expeditions, a Viking leader may have preferred to save his warriors' energy while still collecting loot. Knowing that their reputation preceded them, the Vikings would approach the leader of a community and demand Danegeld, a tribute paid to the Vikings in return for sparing the village, castle, or monastery. Because of the fearsome and abundant stories about Viking brutality, a Danegeld was almost always agreed to. The Northmen would then sail away, pounds of silver or gold richer and with nary a warrior lost or injured, bound for other shores. Although honor-bound to each other, the Vikings were not always true to their word when it came to outsiders. Often they would return to the community they had just left and demand more, threatening attack once again. The frightened residents often would continue to pay the Vikings as many times as they demanded.

VIKING ATTACKS WERE QUICK AND STARTLING IN THEIR FURY

VIKINGS

Vikings didn't want only treasures or slaves; expansion was often a prominent goal. Rather than returning home with their riches, the raiders set up bases in conquered lands from which to launch more attacks. Once a base was established, the Vikings would split into groups and plunder the countryside or sail to nearby lands. Early in the Viking Age, Danish Vikings founded military camps throughout Scotland and nearby islands. From there they attacked England and Ireland, and by 839 they had taken over the whole of Ireland and founded the present-day city of Dublin.

As the Viking Age went on, raids became more and more ambitious. Vikings no longer limited themselves to coastal lands and islands but penetrated deep into Europe, sailing up rivers in their shallow-draft ships. Wide, thick bridges often blocked their path, however, and the Vikings would demand that the locals either raise or remove the bridges to allow them to pass or else face their wrath. As Vikings ventured farther from their homeland, they were more likely to set up winter camps in conquered lands than they were to make the long voyage home.

Some Viking expeditions included women who accompanied their husbands and fathers with the intention of settling in foreign lands. Women were also present in temporary raiding camps. During the winter of 874–75, women made up nearly one-fifth of the population of a Danish Viking camp in England, although evidence suggests that many of the women were British, having either joined the Northmen willingly or been captured. Women played an important role in boosting the morale of the Vikings in the camps, preparing food, caring for the sick or injured, and giving the men a sense of family.

Most Viking battles were fought on land and on foot. The warriors did use horses, often ones they'd commandeered from the enemy, to ride to the battlefields, but then they dismounted and fought hand-to-hand. Agility and speed were essential to the survival of the Viking warrior. He had to be able to dodge, twist, duck, and leap to avoid stabs or strikes from the enemy. Vikings preferred not to fight blade-to-blade in order to preserve the sharpness of their swords; instead, they blocked or turned blows using their shields, then struck with their blades. Vikings were renowned

$\mathcal{T}$he skjaldborg, or shield wall, was a commonly used military tactic among Vikings and other cultures of their time. The skjaldborg was a temporary defense in which warriors overlapped their shields to form a protective wall. The warriors in front knelt, with their shields in front of them, to protect their own chests and the legs of the warriors who stood behind. In this way, the warriors would be protected for a time from the onslaught of javelins or arrows until reinforcements arrived. This tactic originated in ancient fighting cultures such as those of the Romans and Greeks.

for their ferocity in combat, and their enemies did not count on mercy. One particularly gruesome battlefield tactic used by Vikings was called the blood eagle. After capturing or wounding his enemy, a warrior sliced the defeated man's ribcage along his backbone and then pulled out the lungs. The bloody lungs would flap like wings as the victim took his last breaths.

Sea battles were rare, although they were fought on occasion. In such warfare, the Vikings would rope their ships together, lining them up to face the enemy fleet. Some warriors then volleyed arrows at their enemies, while others attempted to board and overtake their ships. Although the Vikings could also set fire to enemy ships, most of the time they chose not to do so, as capturing an intact fleet of ships was more profitable than destroying it.

HORSES WERE OCCASIONALLY RIDDEN INTO BATTLE, BUT MOST VIKINGS PREFERRED TO FIGHT ON THEIR FEET

THE SEAFARING, TERRIFYING, AND ADVENTUROUS

During the long, dark winter months in Scandinavia, skalds recited and embellished stories that told of heroic battles and warriors, instilling excitement in the youth who heard the stories and longed to undertake their own adventures. These stories, called sagas, were passed from generation to generation and accentuated the romantic notion of the fierce Viking warrior. Some Vikings are known only through the sagas, which make their heroics somewhat dubious. However, since many Vikings played a huge role in the history of Europe, their names have become part of European history.

During the early Viking Age, Norway comprised various kingdoms whose chieftains often battled each other for control of land. In 866, Norwegian chieftain Harald Fairhair (c. 860–c. 940) set about toppling rival chieftains and conquering territory. By 872, he had successfully united Norway. Many overthrown Norwegian chief-

tains were not happy under his rule, however, and launched their ships for other coasts.

Rolf the Ganger (c. 870–c. 932) was one such Viking. Although his father was in Harald Fairhair's good graces, Rolf despised the new king. When King Harald issued an order forbidding plundering on Norwegian shores, Rolf left the country to do his ransacking abroad. But when he returned to his homeland, he could not control his hunger for loot and livestock, and he conducted strandhogg on local lands. An angry King Harald called an assembly and declared Rolf an outlaw. Rolf left the country and joined the ninth-century Viking leader Siegfried in his invasion of present-day France.

In 885, Siegfried led a fleet of ships up the Seine River, and on November 25, the Vikings reached Paris. At that time, Paris was a small city on an island in the Seine, and the Vikings wanted only to pass by the town and move farther inland.

SKALD-RECITED STORIES HELPED TO INSPIRE WARRIORS AND WOULD-BE WARRIORS OF ALL AGES IN VIKING CULTURE

$\mathscr{E}$rik Thorvaldsson (c. 950–1003), known as Erik the Red because of his red hair, founded the first Viking settlement in Greenland. Born in Norway, he moved to Iceland with his parents. As a young man, he was exiled for three years as punishment for allegedly killing two men. When he returned from his travels, he told of a land with spectacular blue fjords and green mountains and convinced 400 others to follow him to Greenland, where they established a settlement. His son, Leif Eriksson (c. 970–c. 1020), set off on adventures of his own and became one of the first Europeans to set foot in North America.

However, Parisian bridges blocked their way. Siegfried sought out the **abbot** Joscelin (d. 886), the spiritual leader of Paris, and the two sat down to talk. Siegfried asked that the bridges be raised to allow his Vikings to sail through peacefully. Joscelin, however, refused, having been ordered by Emperor Charles III (839–888) to oppose the Northmen.

Having little choice but to attack, Siegfried and his warriors advanced upon the city with spears in hand and bows and arrows at their shoulders. They used iron picks to hack at the walls of the fortified town and hurled stones over its walls. Parisian defenders poured boiling oil down upon the invaders, and many Vikings fell burning into the river. Still, the Vikings maintained their position, laying siege to the city. No supplies or food were allowed in or out. Disease and **famine** swept through the city, but still the Parisians did not allow the Vikings to pass. In February, the southern bridge, which had been weakened in the attacks, was swept away by floodwaters. Vikings poured through the opened river, but some, angered by the Parisians' resistance, stayed behind to continue the siege. Nearly a year after the siege began, Charles III and his army of French soldiers arrived. But rather than fighting the invaders, the emperor negotiated with them and allowed the bridges to be raised. In addition, he gave the Vikings a large sum of silver and told them they could do what they wished in

THIS ILLUSTRATION SHOWS FRENCH EMPEROR CHARLES III (CENTER) PAYING DANEGELD TO SIEGFRIED'S VIKINGS

the lands beyond Paris; in return, the Vikings promised to retreat by spring.

Not all the Vikings adhered to Charles' wishes, including Rolf the Ganger. Rolf assumed leadership of Viking establishments on the French coast. In 911, French king Charles III (879–929) gave up fighting the Vikings and granted Rolf the region of Normandy under the condition that Rolf become a Christian. Rolf, whose French name was Rollo, agreed and proceeded to marry a Frenchwoman. Normandy, its name derived from "Northman," kept its Viking customs and language for a time. After a few generations, though, it became so integrated with the rest of France that nearly all Viking influence faded from the region.

Sven Forkbeard (c. 960–1014), nicknamed for the distinctive shape of his beard, was a Danish Viking who has lived on in the annals of history. In 994, Sven joined forces with Norwegian Viking Olaf Tryggvason (c. 960–1000) and led a fleet of 94 ships to attack London. The fleet sailed up the River Thames toward London, and when the Vikings reached the city, English king Ethelred (968–1016) gave

IN THE LATE 900S, VIKINGS BEGAN CROSSING THE ENGLISH
CHANNEL TO LAUNCH ATTACKS AGAINST THE CITY OF LONDON

The Viking sagas tell of one Harald Hardrada's legendary feats in battle. According to one story, when the famed
Viking Harald was raiding the Mediterranean island of Sicily, he came upon a town whose fortified walls were too
strong to be breached. Harald noticed birds nesting under the roofs of the town's buildings. Harald captured some of
the birds as they flew out of the town and tied fir branches to their backs and set them on fire. When the birds flew
back to their nests, the thatched roofs caught on fire. Inhabitants fled the burning buildings, and Harald was able to
easily conquer the city.

them Danegeld and arranged a treaty. The treaty, however, did not halt the attacks the Vikings launched upon other parts of England. King Ethelred continued to pay Danegeld until November 1002, when he ordered the murder of all Danes on English soil. Many Danes escaped the massacre, but Sven Forkbeard's sister and her husband were killed. To avenge his sister's murder and the killing of his countrymen, Sven invaded western England. After five years of raids, the Viking chieftain was finally persuaded to withdraw after being paid a Danegeld.

The British were free from large-scale Viking attacks for 2 years until, in 1009, another 11th-century Danish Viking named Thorkell the Tall invaded England. Thorkell's warriors easily defeated the English army that met them. Meanwhile, Sven Forkbeard was readying his forces to launch another attack. By the time Sven attacked in 1013, Thorkell the Tall, whose unit of warriors had broken apart, had joined the army of English king Ethelred II. Even this alliance could not stop Sven, however. In 1014, King Ethelred fled to Normandy, and Sven Forkbeard declared himself king of England.

Sven didn't get to enjoy his kingship for long; his health failed, and he died only a few weeks later. His son Knut the Great (c. 985–1035) took up his sword against remaining pockets of resistance. By this time, Ethelred had also died, and when Ethelred's son and successor died in 1016, there was no one to oppose Knut's reign, and he became king of England for 19 years.

Most Viking warriors were men. However, women accompanied them on many of their expeditions, and some women adopted the warring ways of their male family members. Freydis Eriksdatter (c. 875–?) was the daughter of Erik the Red of Greenland. Fierce and fiery, she refused to sit idly by and watch as her brothers Leif, Thorvald, and Thorstein set off on adventures to Vinland, in present-day North America, where they acquired goods such as grapes and timber that they could trade for great sums. A popular, though likely fictional, saga says that Freydis agreed to accompany two men to Vinland and to split all profits they made from trade. However, when they arrived in Vinland, the ruthless female warrior attacked and killed the two men and their slaves, keeping all the wealth for herself.

AFTER PROLONGED VIKING ASSAULTS ON LONDON (OPPO-SITE), KNUT THE GREAT (ABOVE) TOOK POWER IN ENGLAND

THE SAGAS LIVE ON

By the 11th century, Christianity was sweeping across Scandinavia and replacing the religion of the Old Norse gods. Contact with western European cultures had exposed the Vikings to the Christian faith and customs. Some who had settled in conquered European lands, such as Rolf the Ganger, became Christian like the locals, while other Vikings brought Christianity to Scandinavia when they made their way back home. The new religion spread through the northern countries rather slowly. Many **polytheistic** Scandinavians were reluctant to accept just one god, and some incorporated the worship of Jesus Christ into their rituals for the Norse gods. Christianity only truly took hold as the predominant religion when the Scandinavians' most esteemed leaders adopted the religion themselves and cultivated its growth. In Norway, king Olaf Haraldsson (995–1030), in true Viking fashion, forcefully converted his constituents to Christianity. He gave them three choices: baptism, exile, or death. For his efforts, he was dubbed Saint Olaf, becoming one of Christianity's only Norwegian saints. Other Scandinavian leaders who adopted Christianity included king Harald Bluetooth (c. 910–c. 987) of Denmark and king Olof Skötkonung (c. 980–c. 1022) of Sweden.

Christianity helped to both unify Scandinavian countries and facilitate friendly relations with the Christian kingdoms of western Europe—actions which were in the greater interest of Scandinavian kings. Eliminating wars between chieftains and clans helped to solidify a king's position as leader of the entire country, and peaceful diplomacy and alliances with other countries helped to boost trade, thus generating wealth. Christianity also carried with it an **ideology** of divinely ordained kingship—in other words, kings were called upon by God to lead their countries—which helped the kings maintain power.

OLAF HARALDSSON WAS GIVEN SAINTHOOD A YEAR AFTER HIS DEATH AND DUBBED "NORWAY'S ETERNAL KING"

The unification of Norway, Sweden, and Denmark, and the more peaceable relations with their neighbors, eventually quelled the urge of Vikings to go raiding or exploring. Even so, some Vikings still lusted for land and leadership. Harald Hardrada (1015–1066)—also known as Harald the Ruthless—of Norway had taken to sailing far-off seas, traveling as far east as Kiev in present-day Ukraine and as far south as the Mediterranean. By 1066, Harald desired the throne of England, inspired perhaps by Danish Viking Knut the Great's rule from 1016 to 1035. Harald and his Vikings invaded England but were met by a surprisingly fierce English army at Stamford Bridge.

Harald's army put up a valiant fight but ultimately was defeated, and Harald died in the battle. The English army was weakened by the fray, however, which allowed William, Duke of Normandy, to take over the country in what became known as the Norman Conquest of 1066. Harald's defeat in the Battle of Stamford Bridge signaled the end of the Viking Age, and Harald is often called "The Last Viking."

Viking culture continued to be celebrated in Scandinavia, especially in Iceland, where sagas told of the courage and heroics of Viking warriors, and the **Edda** celebrated myths, rituals, and gods. These stories were told and re-told orally

A DEPICTION OF THE BATTLE OF STAMFORD BRIDGE, ONE OF THE LAST GREAT CLASHES IN THE HISTORY OF THE VIKINGS

In the Viking sagas, the Valkyrie were 12 female spirits who guarded warriors on the battlefield. In the Old Norse language, the word Valkyrie means "chooser of the slain." The Valkyrie are described in the sagas as warrior princesses on horseback; some are beautiful, and others are fierce and grotesque. According to the legends, the Valkyrie would choose who would die in battle. Then the Valkyrie would escort the fallen warriors to Valhalla, an enormous hall in the afterlife reserved for those who died in combat. In Valhalla, the warriors drink mead and prepare for a battle of the gods.

and in great detail, and it was not until the 13th century that many of the sagas were written down. Icelander Snorri Sturluson (1179–1241) was a historian and poet who authored historical texts, such as a history of Norwegian kings, as well as the Prose Edda, a narrative of Norse mythology. Sturluson is also believed to have been the author of *Egil's Saga*, considered one of the greatest Viking sagas. *Egil's Saga* begins in Norway in 850 with Egil's grandfather Kveldulfr, a Viking who plunders his way into wealth. Kveldulfr and his son leave Norway to settle in Iceland, where Egil is born. Egil grows up to become a fierce warrior, killing his first man with a battle-ax at age seven. Although based upon history, *Egil's Saga* assigns many mythical attributes, such as shapeshifting, to its characters. Sturluson's tale of Egil, like others of its time, contributed to the valiant, courageous, and almost superhuman image of the Viking warrior.

Before Sturluson's sagas, the only records of the Vikings were written by Christian monks and historians who had been victimized by Viking raids and thus painted a grim, barbaric picture of the fearsome warriors from the North. In 860, Ermentarius, a French monk, wrote, "Everywhere the Christians are the victims of massacres, burnings, plundering: the Vikings conquer all in their path, and no one resists them." In the 11th century, Dudo, a Norman historian, described the Vikings as "cruel, harsh, destructive, troublesome, wild, ferocious, lustful, lawless, death-dealing, arrogant, ungodly and much else besides." From these descriptions evolved the popular image of a ruthless, heartless warrior.

Many Scandinavians embrace their ancestral past and celebrate the men and women who nearly conquered western Europe. In the 1800s, Viking culture experienced an educational revival; Denmark witnessed the rise of folk high schools in which students learned Viking history and sang patriotic songs about the warriors. Today in Scandinavia, western Europe, and North America, the Viking is remembered through fairs and festivals. Fairgoers wear horned helmets and drink an alcoholic beverage called mead. Battles are re-enacted before cheering crowds. Merchants sell jewelry and rune stones made in the style of Viking culture. Scandinavian settlements across North America, largely concentrated in Minnesota and Wisconsin, and those in Europe, Australia, and New Zealand often boast of their

---

THIS SCOTTISH FESTIVAL INCLUDES COSTUMED "VIKINGS" OF ALL AGES, COMPLETE WITH WEAPONS AND SHIELDS

heritage with signposts and billboards depicting a Viking warrior. The Minnesota Vikings of the National Football League are named in honor of the state's dominant ancestry. The team's logo depicts a blond, mustached warrior, the players' helmets feature painted horns, and the fans embrace their Vikings as ferocious combatants.

Vikings have been celebrated on screen in such movies as 1958's *The Vikings*, starring Kirk Douglas and Tony Curtis, and 1963's *The Long Ships*, based upon Frans Gunnar Bengtsson's historical novel of the same name. *The 13th Warrior*, released in 1999 and starring Antonio Banderas, tells the story of an Arabian messenger who is banished from his homeland and joins a group of Viking warriors as they voyage north to battle mysterious creatures. The 2011 fantasy film *Thor* portrays the hammer-toting Norse god, imagining him being banished from his godly kingdom and

sent to present-day Earth. The Viking warrior has also occasionally played a comedic role in popular culture, such as in the comic strip *Hagar the Horrible*. In the cartoons, Hagar is an overweight, irritable Viking, complete with a red beard and horned helmet, who is often seen traveling in a longship with his sidekick Lucky Eddie. The duo adventure, pillage, and loot, usually with humorous consequences, and return to their homes in an isolated Scandinavian village.

Rather than sinking into oblivion, the Vikings —with their innovative ship designs and their endless resolve to raid, conquer, and settle— have left their mark upon the world. The sagas of these fearsome, fighting men of the North have transcended time to land upon the shores of today's fictional films and books, and the Viking warrior continues to dominate the seas of our imaginations.

THE MINNESOTA VIKINGS HAVE A MASCOT NAMED RAGNAR WHO ENTERS THE STADIUM THROUGH AN INFLATABLE SHIP

In July 2007, in Roskilde, Denmark, 65 sailors of Scandinavian descent boarded a Viking longship called the Sea Stallion *and set sail on a 1,000-mile (1,609 km) journey to Dublin, Ireland, retracing the voyage made by Viking warriors more than 1,000 years earlier. Built using Viking-age tools, the* Sea Stallion *was a 100-foot (30 m) replica of a longship built in 1042. The replica carried some modern equipment the Vikings didn't have, however, such as radios and life jackets. Although the sailors intended to use only wind and rowing power, the* Sea Stallion *had to be towed for 345 miles (555 km) because of bad weather and landed in Dublin 6 weeks after embarking.*

GLOSSARY

abbot—The head or leader of a monastery; in largely Christian communities, the abbot was also often the representative or spokesperson for that community

archaeological—Relating to the discovery or examination of relics of past human life; archaeological findings help explain the lives, activities, and customs of a culture

artisans—People who are skilled at working with their hands at a particular craft such as woodworking

chain mail—A protective suit consisting of thousands of tiny metal loops linked meticulously together

Edda—Either of two 13th-century Icelandic books that narrate legends of mythical gods of the Viking Age

famine—An extreme, extended shortage of food that causes widespread hunger among the people of a region

fjords—Long, narrow inlets of the ocean between cliffs, especially those found along the western coast of Norway

hull—The frame or body of a boat or ship, excluding other parts such as the mast

ideology—A set of beliefs, values, and opinions that shapes the way a person, social group, or political party thinks, acts, and understands the world

illiterate—Unable to read a written language or write in that language

keels—The structural elements of ships that stretch along the center of ships' bottoms from the bow to the stern and help hold the vessel together

migrated—Moved from one country, region, or place to another, often to find food or work

monasteries—Buildings or groups of buildings where monks—usually Christian men who have devoted their lives to God—live and work together

nautical—Relating to ships, sailing, or navigation

pagans—People who hold religious belief in a god or gods other than the Christian, Muslim, or Jewish god

polygamy—The practice of having more than one spouse at a time

polytheistic—Believing in or worshiping more than one god

prow—The forward part of a ship's hull, especially the portion that extends out above the water

self-sustaining—Able to provide for one's own needs, or the needs of a group, independently and without help from others

siege—To attack a fort or castle by surrounding it and threatening the people inside until they are forced to surrender

sledges—Strong, heavy sleds, usually pulled by animals, that transport people or items across snow or ice

tapestry—A heavy piece of cloth with pictures or patterns woven onto it; pictorial designs on tapestries often tell stories or legends

INDEX

BIBLIOGRAPHY

Cohat, Yves. *The Vikings: Lords of the Seas*. New York: Harry N. Abrams, 1992.

Dersin, Denise, ed. *What Life Was Like When Longships Sailed: Vikings AD 800–1100*. Alexandria, Va.: Time-Life Books, 1998.

Graham-Campbell, James, ed. *Cultural Atlas of the Viking World*. New York: Facts on File, 1994.

Haywood, John. *The Penguin Historical Atlas of the Vikings*. New York: The Penguin Group, 1995.

Roesdahl, Else, and David M. Wilson, eds. *From Viking to Crusader: The Scandinavians and Europe 800–1200*. New York: Rizzoli International Publications, 1992.

Sawyer, Peter, ed. *The Oxford Illustrated History of the Vikings*. New York: Oxford University Press, 1997.

Simpson, Jacqueline. *Everyday Life in the Viking Age*. New York: Putnam's, 1969.

Wilson, David. *The Vikings and Their Origins: Scandinavia in the First Millennium*. New York: McGraw-Hill, 1970.